Animal
Partnerships

Written by Kerrie Shanahan

Flying Start
to Literacy®

Contents

A small cleaner wrasse fish is cleaning the mouth of the larger fish.

Introduction

Some animals live most or all their lives in close contact with an animal from another species. This ongoing relationship between different types of animals is called a symbiotic relationship.

Why would animals do this? Why would they spend their whole life with another type of animal? Most animals do it because they get something out of the relationship. They might get an easy meal, protection, shelter or help with grooming.

There are different types of animal partnerships. In some partnerships, both animals benefit. In others, one animal benefits and the other isn't affected in either a good or bad way. But sometimes, one animal benefits while the other is harmed. This is good for the one, but bad for the other.

The world is full of weird and wonderful animal partnerships!

This oxpecker is picking ticks off the buffalo. The oxpecker eats the ticks and this helps the buffalo.

Chapter 1 Win-win

Sometimes, both animals in a partnership benefit by living together. This type of relationship is called a mutualistic relationship.

Both animals in the partnership have one or more of their needs met. They might get food, shelter or protection from **predators**, or they might be cleaned by the other animal, which helps them stay healthy.

▲ A goby fish and shrimp live side by side.

▶ Clown fish and sea anemones live together.

Here are some examples of animals that benefit from living together:

- clown fish and sea anemones

- caterpillars and ants

- shrimp and goby fish.

How do these relationships work?

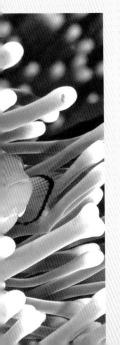

▲ These weaver ants are protecting a caterpillar.

Clown fish and sea anemones

You've probably seen images of stripy clown fish zipping in and out of the long tentacles of a sea anemone. These two animals live together, which benefits both of them.

Sea anemones are animals that attach themselves to rocks or coral. They have long tentacles that can sting and trap small fish and other sea animals that they then eat.

Clown fish shelter in the tentacles of sea anemones and use them as protection. Predators that might want to eat a clown fish will not risk getting stung by the sea anemone's poisonous tentacles. They leave the clown fish alone.

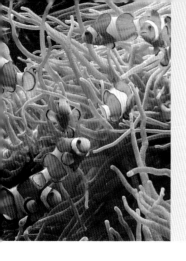

Do you wonder why?

A sea anemone doesn't have eyes, so how does it know not to sting and eat the clown fish? The clown fish has slimy **mucus** on its body. Because of this mucus, the sea anemone doesn't recognise it as food, and so it doesn't release its **venom** to sting it.

The clown fish is good for the sea anemone, too. The clown fish keeps the sea anemone clean by eating up any leftover food or algae that is growing on it. Clown fish also help the sea anemone by chasing away predators that might want to eat it.

This is a win–win partnership!

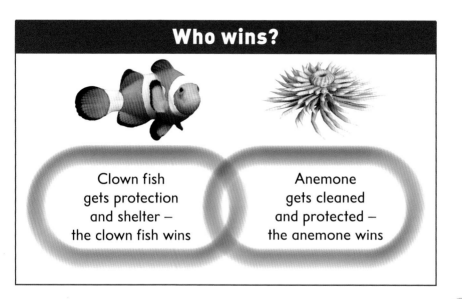

Who wins?

Clown fish gets protection and shelter – the clown fish wins

Anemone gets cleaned and protected – the anemone wins

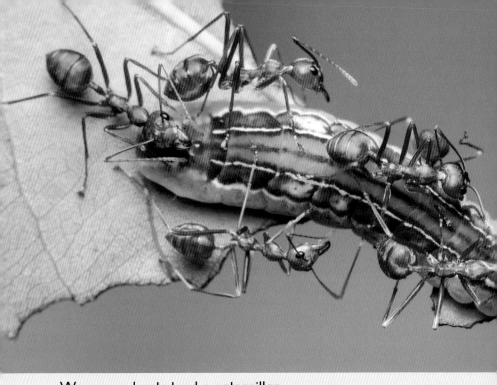

Weaver red ants tend a caterpillar.

Caterpillars and ants

Have you ever heard of ants that protect caterpillars? Well, it does happen. And these particular ants and caterpillars would not survive without each other. This partnership is an example of a fairly common type of symbiotic relationship, in which one animal gets protection and the other gets food.

These caterpillars secrete a special sugary substance for the ants to eat. The ants protect the caterpillar from predators such as wasps and bugs that want to eat it. They attack and scare away these killers to keep the caterpillar safe.

One type of caterpillar has even developed a noise that it makes when it needs protecting. When it makes this noise, the ants come running and they attack. They know they must protect the caterpillar . . . and their food!

Both animals are winners in this partnership.

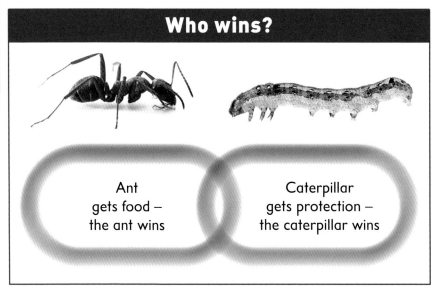

Who wins?

| Ant gets food – the ant wins | Caterpillar gets protection – the caterpillar wins |

Did you know?
Some ants have a partnership with insects called aphids:
- The aphids produce a type of sweet waste called honeydew, which the ants eat.
- The ants protect the aphids from predators.

Shrimp and goby fish

Deep in the ocean, a shrimp is busily digging a burrow in the sandy seafloor. When it has finished digging, it will hide inside the burrow, safe from larger fish that are looking for a meal.

The shrimp, which is nearly blind, carries the sand it has dug to deposit outside the burrow. This is dangerous work! Swimming above are fish looking for their next meal.

Hovering just outside the burrow is a slender orange goby fish. It is watching the shrimp closely. Is this the end for the hardworking shrimp? Luckily, the goby fish doesn't eat the shrimp. Instead, it swims above it in a protective manner.

The goby fish and the shrimp live side by side in a burrow.

When a large fish swims by, the goby fish starts frantically swishing its tail back and forth, tapping against the shrimp's antennae. Danger! Danger!

Thanks to the goby fish, the shrimp knows to hide. It scurries back into the safety of the burrow.

The danger is gone for now, so the shrimp zips back outside and resumes digging. And the goby fish continues to stand guard, looking out for danger.

When the burrow is finally finished, the shrimp retreats inside. So too does the goby fish. The shrimp shares its new burrow with its bodyguard, the goby fish.

What a partnership!

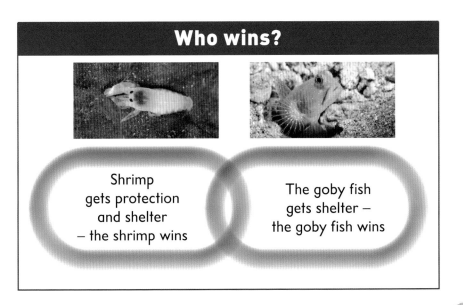

Who wins?

Shrimp gets protection and shelter – the shrimp wins

The goby fish gets shelter – the goby fish wins

Chapter 2
One winner, no loser

Sometimes, when two animals live together, only one animal benefits. It gets one or more of its needs met such as food, protection, shelter or a way of moving around.

The other animal in the relationship isn't affected. It doesn't get anything positive from the relationship, but there aren't any major negatives, either. This is called commensalism.

▼ A hummingbird

▲ A remora fish

Here are some animals that live together. Only one of them benefits from the relationship, while the other animal is not harmed:

- hummingbirds and flower mites

- remora fish and sharks

- whales and barnacles.

▶ This humpback whale is covered in barnacles.

Hummingbirds and flower mites

Some animals are great movers. They run, fly, swim or hop from one place to another. But other animals aren't so great at moving. So how do these animals get around? Well, some hitch a ride with another animal!

Flower mites are tiny eight-legged creatures that feed on the nectar and pollen of flowers. They can walk from flower to flower on one plant, but if they need to get to flowers on another plant, it's too far for these small creatures to walk.

When the hummingbird puts its beak in a flower, the flower mite crawls up its nostril and gets a ride to the next flower.

This tiny, red mite eats flower pollen and nectar. It's a long walk to the next flower.

Amazingly, the flower mite catches a ride inside a nostril of the hummingbird. The hummingbird also eats nectar, and it flies from plant to plant doing so. The flower mite gets transported straight to its food source.

The flower mite benefits from this partnership. The hummingbird doesn't benefit, but it isn't greatly affected, either. The mite drinks nectar, but there is still enough for the hummingbird, too!

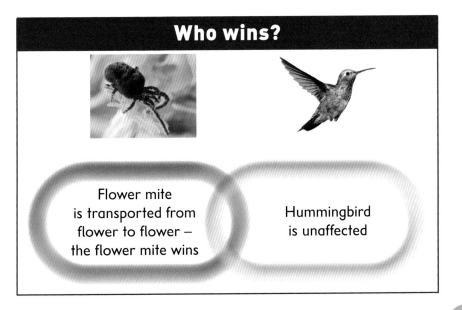

Who wins?

Flower mite is transported from flower to flower – the flower mite wins

Hummingbird is unaffected

These remora fish are hitching a ride with a whale shark.

Remora fish and sharks

When an animal moves from one place to another, it uses lots of energy. So if an animal can save this energy, then why not? It's a big benefit for the creature.

The remora fish is a saltwater fish that lives in warm ocean waters all around the world. It has an interesting way of getting around in the ocean. It attaches itself to a shark!

Typically, a fish has a fin on top of its body. But the fin on top of the remora fish looks very different. It has adapted into a flat oval-shaped **sucker**. It looks a bit like the sole of a shoe.

Close-up of the sucker on a remora fish

When a remora fish uses this sucker to stick onto the shark's back, it is upside down. The fish gets a free ride, and therefore saves a lot of energy. It is also thought that the fish eats leftover food scraps from its **host**.

What does the shark get out of this partnership? Nothing! But having a small remora fish on its back doesn't greatly affect the shark either. It may slow the shark down a tiny bit, but not enough to be a problem.

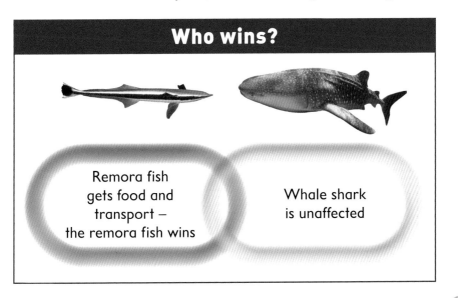

Who wins?

Remora fish gets food and transport – the remora fish wins

Whale shark is unaffected

Whales and barnacles

Whales cover large distances as they swim through ocean waters. Adult barnacles are small sea animals that can't move – not without the help of a whale!

Barnacles produce eggs that turn into larvae. During this stage of life they swim around freely. But when they develop into adults, they cannot move.

So when it is time to become an adult, the larvae land on a whale. They then use their antennae to find a place on the whale that gets good water flow, such as the whale's head or front fins.

As the barnacle larvae develop into adults, they create tube-shaped holes on their underside. Gradually, the whale's skin is pulled up into these holes as it grows.

The whale's skin continues to grow and fills up the holes. The barnacle is stuck firmly to the whale for the rest of its life.

Did you know?
There are over 1,000 species of barnacles. Each species lives only on a particular species of whale.

This humpback whale has barnacles growing on its head.

But why do barnacles do this? Whales eat plankton, which are tiny organisms that float in the water. Barnacles eat plankton, too. So when a whale swims through a patch of plankton, the barnacles get an easy meal along with the free ride. The whales get nothing positive from the barnacles living on them, but they aren't affected in a negative way, either.

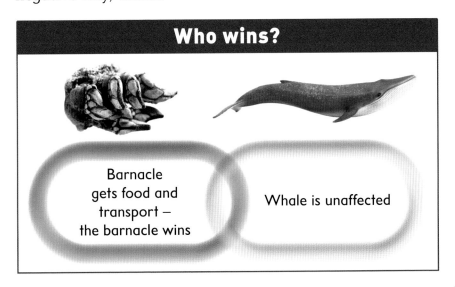

Who wins?

Barnacle gets food and transport – the barnacle wins

Whale is unaffected

Chapter 3

One winner, one loser

Not all animal partnerships are good for both animals. Sometimes, when one animal wins, the other animal loses. This type of relationship is called a parasitic relationship.

The animal that benefits is the winner. It is called the **parasite**. The animal that the parasite lives on is the loser. It is called the **host**. The host is affected in a negative way by the relationship. It can become injured or sick, or even die because of the partnership.

▲ A tick

▼ The caterpillar of the large blue butterfly is a parasite

One animal in a parasitic relationship needs the partnership, but the other animal definitely does not.

Each of these animals couldn't survive without the animal it lives with:

- ticks

- parasitic caterpillars

- some flatworms.

▲ This snail's eyestalks are swollen with the larvae of a flatworm.

Ticks

Ticks are small animals that feed on the blood of other animals. They are found all around the world in forests and woodland areas.

Ticks attach themselves to a host – an animal such as a dog, horse, deer, rat or bird. Some types of ticks then feed nonstop on their host's blood.

This relationship is great for the tick because it has a constant food supply and a place to live. But the relationship is damaging for the host.

A vet removes a tick from a dog's ear.

A tick crawls on a blade of grass. Ticks are small and hard to see.

The tick can hurt the host and can even cause death. The tick doesn't want this to happen – it needs a live host so that it can continue living there. But sometimes, the tick drinks too much, or it might secrete **venom** into its host. This venom damages the host's nerves and causes paralysis and sometimes death.

This is a one-sided animal partnership where only the tick wins.

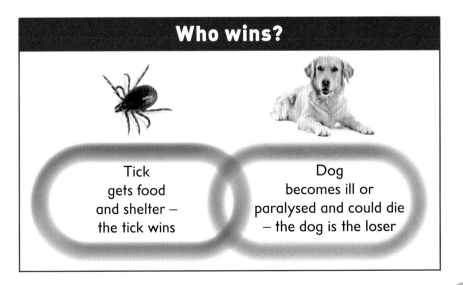

Who wins?

Tick
gets food
and shelter –
the tick wins

Dog
becomes ill or
paralysed and could die
– the dog is the loser

Blue butterfly caterpillars and ants

Some caterpillars and ants have a positive partnership in which both animals help each other survive. But there is one type of caterpillar that is an enemy to a certain type of red ant. And the ant doesn't know it! The caterpillar is an enemy in disguise.

The caterpillar of the large blue butterfly pretends to be an ant so that it can get inside the nest of the red ants. How does it do this? The caterpillar releases a scent and makes sounds that trick the ants into thinking it is an ant larvae. The ants then carry the caterpillar back to their nest, thinking they are taking one of their own young ants back home.

This red ant is moving an ant grub to safety.

This red ant is carrying the caterpillar of the blue butterfly, which looks like the red ant grub.

Once the caterpillar is in the nest, it eats the ant larvae. The caterpillar even copies the sounds made by the queen ant so that the adult ants leave it alone. It can then eat as many young ants as it pleases. The caterpillar stays in the nest for almost a year, until it is ready to transform into a butterfly.

This is a great partnership for the caterpillar, but definitely not good for the ants!

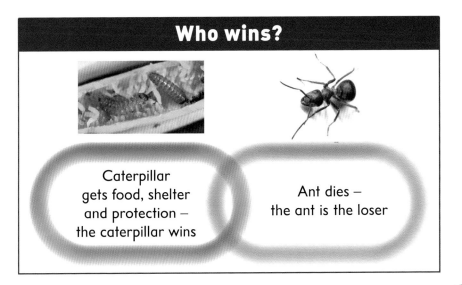

Who wins?

Caterpillar gets food, shelter and protection – the caterpillar wins

Ant dies – the ant is the loser

Flatworms and snails

One type of tiny flatworm has an incredible parasitic relationship with snails. The relationship is great for the flatworm, but a disaster for the snail! It begins when a snail eats the eggs of the flatworm. The flatworm's eggs hatch inside the snail.

After hatching, the flatworm larvae move into the snail's eyestalks, where they grow bigger and bigger. The larvae grow so big that the snail's thin eyestalks become swollen. They look like wriggling worms or caterpillars – the perfect food for a bird. When a bird sees the snail, it gobbles it up – with the flatworm larvae inside it!

Inside the bird, the flatworm larvae develop into adults and reproduce, creating eggs. When the bird leaves its droppings on a plant, the droppings are full of flatworm eggs. When a snail eats the bird droppings that contain flatworm eggs, the cycle begins all over again.

Can you believe it?

Flatworms inside a snail infect the snail's brain. This causes the snail to climb towards the sunlight, where it is easily seen by birds. Normally, snails stay hidden in the shade, out of sight!

The eyestalks on this snail are swollen with the flatworm larvae.

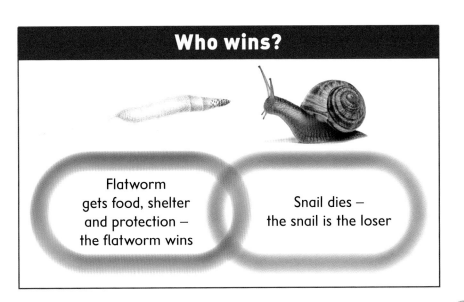

Who wins?

Flatworm gets food, shelter and protection – the flatworm wins

Snail dies – the snail is the loser

Conclusion

Some animals live most of their lives with an animal from another species because living in this way helps to meet their needs. These symbiotic relationships are important for both animals involved.

But these partnerships are also important to other animals and plants that live close by. The way the animals in these partnerships behave helps to keep their ecosystem healthy.

Animal partnerships are not only fascinating, they play a key role in maintaining a balanced ecosystem.

Glossary

host a living animal or plant on which another animal lives

mucus a slippery liquid produced by an animal; this liquid protects the animal

parasite a living animal or plant that lives off another animal

predators animals that kill other animals for food

sucker a part that some animals have that they can use to attach to other animals

venom a poison that is produced by an animal; it is used to paralyse or kill other animals

Index